Impact of Digital Overload on Health and Society

C. P. Kumar

Impact of Digital Overload on Health and Society

C. P. Kumar
Reiki Healer
Roorkee - 247667, India

Disclaimer

While every effort has been made to ensure the accuracy and completeness of the content in this book, the author cannot guarantee that the information contained herein is error-free, up-to-date, or suitable for every individual circumstance.

The author shall not be held liable or responsible for any errors or omissions in the content of the book, nor for any damages, or losses that may arise from any actions taken based upon the suggestions or contents presented in the book.

Readers are advised to use their own judgment and discretion in applying the information provided in this book, and to consult with qualified professionals before taking any action based on the contents of this book. The author disclaims any and all liability or responsibility for any actions taken or not taken based on the information contained in this book.

DEDICATION

To those captivated by the digital tide,

This book is dedicated to those who navigate the currents of the digital age. Within these chapters, we unravel the evolution of electronic gadgets, explore the allure of technology, and confront the impact on health and society.

From vision strains to sedentary lifestyles, we dissect the consequences of excessive device use. Repetitive strain injuries and digital distractions are exposed, urging us to find balance amid the chaos.

We delve into the realms of mental well-being, social media's sway on self-esteem, and the dark corners of cyberbullying. Parenthood in the digital age and the erosion of face-to-face connections are examined, and love's digital journey is mapped.

Tech's role in health, government initiatives, and strategies for digital well-being are spotlighted, offering paths to a more harmonious coexistence.

To all seeking harmony in this digital era, this dedication is a beacon. May the insights within guide you toward healthier tech habits and a more balanced future.

With gratitude,

C. P. Kumar

CONTENTS

PREFACE

In the tapestry of our modern existence, the threads of technology are woven intricately, binding us to an era of unparalleled advancement and unforeseen complexities. The digital revolution, a symphony of innovation and transformation, has ushered in a new age where the rhythmic pulses of electronic devices have become the backdrop to our lives. Yet, amidst this crescendo of progress, a hushed question lingers: What toll does this unceasing digital symphony exact on our health and the social fabric we hold dear?

This book, "Impact of Digital Overload on Health and Society," embarks on an illuminating voyage into uncharted waters, guiding us through the labyrinthine realms of our digital landscape. In this exploration, we delve beyond the glossy veneer of screens and circuits, seeking to unveil the intricate dance between technology and the well-being of both individuals and communities.

Our journey begins with an exploration of the roots of our electronic age, tracing the relentless evolution of gadgets that now permeate every corner of our lives. From the humble beginnings to the ubiquitous marvels they have become, we uncover the transformation that has shaped the very essence of our world.

Yet, our fascination with technology transcends mere utility. It tugs at the strings of our psychology, weaving a compelling narrative that entices us to indulge in excessive device usage. As we uncover the psychological underpinnings, we unveil the allure that keeps us tethered to our screens, often at the expense of our own well-being.

This journey goes beyond our senses, revealing how prolonged exposure to screens impacts our vision, and how the intimate connection between technology and our physical health reveals itself in sedentary lifestyles and the specter of obesity.

The subtle dangers that lurk in the digital realm emerge as we confront the risks of repetitive strain injuries, serving as a stark reminder that our interactions with technology can have far-reaching implications for our physicality.

However, the story does not end at the individual level. Society grapples with a pervasive epidemic of digital distraction, eroding our ability to concentrate and undermining productivity. As the line between work and leisure blurs, we dissect the mental toll of constant connectivity, exposing the very real specter of burnout in an always-on world.

In the midst of this maelstrom, we traverse the spectrum of escapism and mental well-being, dissect the complex interplay between social media and self-esteem, and confront the shadowy dimensions of cyberbullying and digital harassment. We explore how the digital transformation shapes the landscape of parenting and unravels the threads of face-to-face communication, all while examining the intricate dynamics of love and relationships in an age defined by screens.

However, as we navigate the labyrinthine impact of technology, we also discover pathways to balance and well-being. We turn our gaze toward the tech industry's role, scrutinize government policies, and unearth initiatives that seek to detoxify our digital lives.

This journey, while marked by challenges, is ultimately a journey of hope and empowerment. "Impact of Digital Overload on Health and Society" beckons you to embark on this odyssey, to question the digital age's influence on our health and society, and to emerge armed with insights that empower us to reclaim control over our technological destinies. As you flip these pages, may the revelations within kindle a transformation – one that ushers in an era where technology harmonizes with well-being, and where the digital symphony enriches, rather than overwhelms, our lives.

C. P. Kumar
Reiki Healer
Former Scientist 'G', National Institute of Hydrology
Roorkee - 247667, India
E-mail: cpkumar@yahoo.com
Web: https://www.angelfire.com/nh/cpkumar/virgo.html

Chapter 1. The Digital Revolution
Understanding the Evolution of Electronic Gadgets and Their Ubiquity

Introduction

In the last few decades, the world has witnessed an unprecedented transformation driven by technological advancements, commonly referred to as the digital revolution. This revolution has profoundly impacted various aspects of our lives, from communication and entertainment to work and education. One of the most remarkable outcomes of this revolution is the proliferation of electronic gadgets. These gadgets have become an integral part of our daily routines, contributing to the phenomenon of digital overload. This article delves into the evolution of electronic gadgets, their increasing ubiquity, and the implications of this digital revolution on health and society.

The Genesis of Electronic Gadgets

1. The Dawn of Electronics

The roots of electronic gadgets can be traced back to the late 19th and early 20th centuries when pioneers like Thomas Edison and Nikola Tesla laid the groundwork for modern electronics. Their inventions, such as the electric light bulb and alternating current (AC) power systems, paved the way for the development of more sophisticated electronic devices.

A pivotal moment in the evolution of electronics came with the invention of the transistor in 1947 by John Bardeen, Walter Brattain, and William Shockley. Transistors, which replaced bulky vacuum tubes, marked a significant leap forward in miniaturization and energy efficiency. This breakthrough paved the way for the creation of integrated circuits, commonly known as computer chips, which led to the development of smaller and more powerful electronic devices.

The Evolution of Electronic Gadgets

1. From Brick Phones to Smartphones

The evolution of communication gadgets has been particularly striking. The first mobile phones were cumbersome "brick" devices primarily used for voice communication. However, with the advent of digital cellular networks, the 1980s saw the rise of more compact and functional mobile phones. The true revolution, however, arrived with the introduction of smartphones in the early 2000s, combining telephony with computing capabilities and internet access.

2. Computing On the Go

The evolution of computing gadgets has witnessed the transformation from large mainframe computers to portable laptops and tablets. Laptops, with their compact design and built-in battery, allowed users to take their work on the go. Tablets, on the other hand, introduced a new form factor with touch interfaces, making computing more intuitive and accessible.

3. The Entertainment Frontier

The way we consume entertainment has also been revolutionized by electronic gadgets. The Walkman, introduced by Sony in the late 1970s, brought music on the move. This was followed by portable CD players and, eventually, digital music players like the iPod. The proliferation of smartphones further consolidated music playback into a single device. In the realm of video entertainment, devices like DVD players evolved into streaming devices that provide instant access to a vast array of multimedia content.

4. Beyond Communication and Entertainment

The digital revolution has expanded the role of electronic gadgets beyond communication and entertainment. The concept of the Internet of Things (IoT) emerged, connecting everyday objects to the internet and enabling them to collect and exchange data. Smart home devices, wearable fitness trackers, and even connected kitchen appliances exemplify the potential of IoT gadgets to enhance convenience and efficiency in various aspects of life.

Ubiquity and Its Implications

1. The Ubiquitous Nature of Electronic Gadgets

The ubiquity of electronic gadgets is undeniable. A walk through any urban environment reveals countless individuals engrossed in their smartphones, earbuds in place, and smartwatches adorning their wrists. The omnipresence of these gadgets highlights their integration into the fabric of modern society.

2. Societal Transformations and Challenges

The widespread adoption of electronic gadgets has brought about transformative societal changes. Communication has become instantaneous, breaking down geographical barriers and enabling global connections. Information is readily accessible, empowering individuals with knowledge at their fingertips. However, this constant connectivity has also raised concerns about privacy, data security, and the blurring of boundaries between work and personal life.

3. Health Implications of Digital Overload

As electronic gadgets have become an integral part of daily life, concerns about their impact on physical and mental health have grown. The phenomenon of digital overload, characterized by excessive screen time, information overload, and constant notifications, has been linked to various health issues. Prolonged gadget use has been associated with digital eye strain, disrupted sleep patterns, and a decline in face-to-face social interactions.

4. Navigating the Digital Landscape Mindfully

While the digital revolution has undoubtedly enhanced our lives in numerous ways, it is essential to navigate this landscape mindfully. Establishing healthy usage patterns, setting boundaries for screen time, and incorporating digital detox routines can help mitigate the negative effects of digital overload. Additionally, promoting digital literacy and educating individuals about responsible gadget use can empower them to make informed choices.

Conclusion

The evolution and ubiquity of electronic gadgets are undeniable hallmarks of the digital revolution. From humble beginnings rooted in early electronics to the sophisticated devices that now define modern life, these gadgets have reshaped the way we communicate, work, and entertain ourselves. While the convenience and connectivity they offer are undeniable, it is crucial to strike a balance between their benefits and potential drawbacks. As society continues to grapple with the implications of digital overload, fostering a culture of mindful gadget use and embracing the transformative power of technology can pave the way for a healthier and more harmonious coexistence between humans and their electronic companions.

Chapter 2. The Allure of Technology
Exploring the Psychology Behind Excessive Device Usage

Introduction

In the digital age, technology has become an integral part of our lives, transforming the way we communicate, work, and entertain ourselves. However, the unprecedented proliferation of devices and screens has given rise to a phenomenon known as digital overload. This article delves into the intricate interplay of psychology and technology, shedding light on why individuals find themselves ensnared in excessive device usage. Understanding the underlying psychological mechanisms is crucial for comprehending the impact of digital overload on health and society.

The Pull of Instant Gratification

1. Dopamine and Reward Pathways

The allure of technology can be attributed, in part, to the brain's reward system. Dopamine, often referred to as the "feel-good" neurotransmitter, plays a pivotal role in shaping human behavior by reinforcing pleasurable experiences. When individuals engage with technology, such as receiving notifications or likes on social media, dopamine is released, creating a sense of pleasure and satisfaction.

2. Instant Gratification and Device Usage

The instant gratification offered by technology taps into our evolutionary instincts. Throughout history, our ancestors developed a preference for quick rewards to survive in a challenging environment. In the modern context, this preference manifests as the constant need to check devices for updates, notifications, and messages.

3. The Feedback Loop of Dopamine

The intermittent nature of rewards, such as new emails or notifications, triggers a dopamine feedback loop that keeps individuals engaged with their devices. This cycle of anticipation, reward, and desire for more contributes to the compulsive nature of device usage, making it challenging to break free from the grasp of technology.

Escapism and Digital Realms

1. Escapism in the Digital Age

The allure of technology also lies in its ability to provide an escape from the challenges and stressors of everyday life. Digital platforms offer a virtual realm where individuals can momentarily disconnect from reality and immerse themselves in a world of their choosing. This form of escapism can provide relief from anxiety, boredom, and emotional distress.

2. The Appeal of Virtual Environments

Virtual environments, such as social media, online games, and virtual reality, offer a sense of autonomy, anonymity, and control. In these spaces, individuals can curate their identity, connect with like-minded individuals, and engage in novel experiences that may be lacking in their offline lives.

3. FOMO and Social Comparison

Fear of Missing Out (FOMO) and the tendency to compare oneself with others play a significant role in excessive device usage. Social media platforms present carefully curated images of people's lives, leading to feelings of inadequacy and the desire to stay constantly connected to avoid missing out on experiences.

The Psychological Impact of Device Dependence

1. Digital Dopamine Dependence

Excessive device usage can lead to a form of digital dopamine dependence, where individuals rely on their devices for mood regulation and emotional well-being. The absence of device-related rewards can result in withdrawal symptoms akin to substance addiction.

2. Reduced Attention Span and Cognitive Load

The constant stream of information and notifications contributes to reduced attention span and cognitive load. The brain's ability to focus on tasks is compromised, impacting productivity and overall cognitive functioning.

3. Negative Social Comparisons and Self-Esteem

Excessive device usage can lead to negative social comparisons, fostering feelings of insecurity and low self-esteem. Constant exposure to idealized images on social media can create unrealistic standards and lead to a distorted self-perception.

Navigating Toward Digital Well-Being

1. Mindful Device Usage

Developing mindfulness around device usage involves becoming aware of one's motivations and emotions when engaging with technology. Practicing mindful device usage can help individuals regain control over their digital habits and reduce the compulsion to constantly check devices.

2. Setting Boundaries and Digital Detox

Establishing clear boundaries for device usage, such as designated screen-free times or zones, can help individuals strike a healthier balance between their online and offline lives. Periodic digital detoxes can provide an opportunity to reset and reevaluate one's relationship with technology.

3. Cultivating Real-World Connections

Fostering meaningful face-to-face interactions and connections can counteract the isolating effects of excessive device usage. Spending quality time with loved ones and engaging in activities that promote human connection can contribute to overall well-being.

Conclusion

The allure of technology and its impact on excessive device usage are deeply rooted in the complex interplay of psychology and human behavior. The instant gratification provided by technology, the allure of virtual realms, and the psychological consequences of device dependence all contribute to the digital overload experienced by many. As society continues to evolve in the digital era, understanding these underlying psychological mechanisms is essential for promoting digital well-being and mitigating the negative effects of digital overload on both individual health and societal harmony. By recognizing the psychological triggers and fostering mindful device usage, individuals can navigate the digital landscape with greater intentionality and balance, ensuring a healthier relationship with technology in an increasingly connected world.

Introduction

In today's digital age, we find ourselves constantly immersed in a world of screens - from smartphones and tablets to computers and televisions. While these devices have undoubtedly revolutionized the way we live and communicate, there is growing concern about their potential impact on our health, particularly on our vision. This article delves into the effects of screen time on eye health, exploring the various ways gadgets can influence our eyes and offering practical tips to mitigate potential risks.

Understanding the Digital Age and Screen Time

1. The Rise of Screen Time

The advent of the digital era has brought about an unprecedented surge in screen time. From work-related tasks to leisure activities, screens have become an integral part of our daily lives. With the proliferation of smartphones and the ubiquity of computers, it's not uncommon for individuals to spend several hours each day staring at screens.

2. Types of Screens and Their Impact

Different screens emit varying levels of light, and the impact on eye health can differ. LED-backlit screens, commonly found in smartphones and computers, emit blue light, which has been linked to potential eye strain and discomfort. E-readers and tablets, on the other hand, often use e-ink technology, which is considered less harsh on the eyes.

Effects of Screen Time on Eye Health

1. Digital Eye Strain

Prolonged screen time can lead to digital eye strain, a condition characterized by symptoms such as dry eyes, headaches, blurred vision, and discomfort. The phenomenon is often exacerbated by factors like poor lighting, improper screen positioning, and inadequate blinking.

2. Blue Light and Sleep Disruption

Blue light emitted by screens can disrupt our sleep-wake cycle by suppressing the production of melatonin, a hormone that regulates sleep. This disruption not only affects the quality of sleep but also has cascading effects on overall health and well-being.

3. Myopia and Screen Time

Recent research suggests a correlation between increased screen time and the development of myopia (nearsightedness), especially among children and adolescents. Prolonged focusing on nearby objects, such as screens, may contribute to the elongation of the eyeball, leading to vision problems.

Mitigating the Effects of Screen Time on Eye Health

1. The 20-20-20 Rule

A simple yet effective strategy to reduce digital eye strain is the 20-20-20 rule. Every 20 minutes, take a 20-second break and focus on an object at least 20 feet away. This practice helps alleviate the strain on the eye's focusing muscles and encourages regular blinking.

2. Blue Light Filters and Screen Settings

Many devices offer blue light filters that can be activated to reduce the amount of blue light emitted. Additionally, adjusting screen settings such as brightness and contrast can help create a more comfortable viewing experience, particularly in low-light environments.

3. Ergonomics and Screen Positioning

Proper ergonomics play a crucial role in reducing eye strain. Position your screen at eye level and maintain a comfortable viewing distance to minimize the need for excessive focusing and squinting.

4. Outdoor Time and Myopia Prevention

Encouraging outdoor activities and spending time in natural light has been associated with a reduced risk of myopia development, particularly in children. Outdoor time helps the eyes focus on distant objects and may help counteract the effects of prolonged near-work activities.

Future Considerations and Conclusion

1. Technological Innovations and Eye Health

As technology continues to evolve, so do efforts to address its potential impact on eye health. Innovations such as improved screen materials, adjustable lighting systems, and augmented reality interfaces aim to provide more comfortable and less strenuous visual experiences.

2. Balancing Screen Time and Health

The key to maintaining good eye health in the digital age lies in striking a balance between screen time and healthy practices. By incorporating regular breaks, proper lighting, and outdoor activities, we can mitigate the negative effects of screen exposure on our vision.

3. Conclusion: Navigating the Digital Era Mindfully

While screens have undoubtedly transformed the way we live and interact, it is essential to approach our digital habits mindfully. By being aware of the potential effects of screen time on our vision and taking proactive steps to protect our eyes, we can fully embrace the benefits of technology without compromising our long-term eye health.

In an age where screens dominate our daily routines, understanding and managing the impact of screen time on our eyes is crucial. By implementing practical strategies and fostering a healthy relationship with technology, we can navigate the digital era while safeguarding our precious vision.

Chapter 4. Sedentary Lifestyle and Obesity
Unraveling the Link between Excessive Device Use and Physical Inactivity

Introduction

In the modern digital age, the proliferation of devices and the rapid integration of technology into our daily lives have brought unprecedented convenience and connectivity. However, this convenience comes at a cost, as the sedentary lifestyle resulting from excessive device use has emerged as a significant health concern. In this article, we delve into the intricate relationship between sedentary behavior, obesity, and the rampant use of digital devices. We will explore the mechanisms through which prolonged screen time contributes to physical inactivity and weight gain, shedding light on the broader impact of digital overload on health and society.

The Sedentary Epidemic

1. Defining Sedentary Behavior

Sedentary behavior is characterized by activities involving low energy expenditure, such as sitting or lying down, often accompanied by screen-based interactions. The digital revolution has led to a surge in sedentary behaviors, with individuals spending extended periods engaged in activities like scrolling through social media, watching videos, and playing games on various devices.

2. Prevalence of Sedentary Lifestyle

The prevalence of sedentary behavior has reached alarming levels globally. The increased accessibility and affordability of digital devices have contributed to a reduction in physical activity and a rise in screen time among people of all ages. This trend has profound implications for public health, particularly in terms of obesity and related health issues.

Unraveling the Mechanisms

1. Impact on Physical Activity

Excessive device use often displaces active pursuits, leading to decreased engagement in physical activities such as sports, walking, or even routine household chores. The convenience of digital entertainment and work-related tasks encourages prolonged sitting, further exacerbating the decline in physical activity levels.

2. Psychosocial Factors

The allure of digital devices lies not only in their functionality but also in the sense of connection and satisfaction they provide. The dopamine-driven reward system associated with app notifications and social media engagement can lead to addictive behavior, encouraging individuals to remain sedentary while seeking digital gratification.

3. Disruption of Circadian Rhythms

Extended screen time, especially during evening hours, can disrupt circadian rhythms (the natural, approximately 24-hour cycles that regulate various physiological and behavioral processes in living organisms) and interfere with sleep patterns. Poor sleep quality and insufficient sleep duration have been linked to weight gain and obesity. The interplay between screen exposure, disrupted sleep, and weight-related issues highlights a complex web of factors contributing to the sedentary-obesity link.

Sedentary Lifestyle and Obesity

1. Caloric Imbalance

Sedentary behavior not only reduces energy expenditure but can also lead to an increase in caloric intake. Mindless snacking while engrossed in digital activities often goes unnoticed, contributing to an energy surplus that can result in weight gain over time.

2. Metabolic Consequences

Prolonged periods of sitting have been associated with adverse metabolic changes, including insulin resistance and altered glucose metabolism. These physiological alterations can promote the development of obesity and increase the risk of type 2 diabetes.

3. Fat Accumulation and Muscle Atrophy

A sedentary lifestyle can lead to a decline in muscle mass and an increase in fat accumulation, particularly around the abdominal region. Muscle atrophy and reduced muscle activity contribute to a decrease in overall metabolic rate, making weight management even more challenging.

Addressing the Issue

1. Promoting Physical Activity

Encouraging regular physical activity is paramount in mitigating the negative effects of a sedentary lifestyle. Public health campaigns, workplace wellness initiatives, and educational programs can raise awareness about the importance of staying active and provide strategies to incorporate movement into daily routines.

2. Digital Detox and Screen Time Management

Implementing digital detox periods and setting screen time limits can help individuals regain control over their device use. By consciously reducing screen time and engaging in alternative leisure activities, individuals can break the cycle of sedentary behavior.

3. Ergonomics and Active Workstations

Redesigning work environments to promote movement and incorporating active workstations can combat the sedentary nature of many jobs. Sit-stand desks, walking meetings, and opportunities for short exercise breaks can help counteract the negative effects of prolonged sitting.

A Holistic Approach to Wellness

1. Mindfulness and Intentionality

Practicing mindfulness and cultivating awareness of one's digital habits can facilitate a more intentional and balanced approach to device use. Mindful screen time can help individuals make conscious choices and strike a healthier equilibrium between technology and physical activity.

Fostering social connections and community engagement can provide alternatives to screen-based interactions. Group activities, sports, and outdoor events not only promote physical activity but also contribute to emotional well-being and a sense of belonging.

Conclusion

The sedentary lifestyle facilitated by excessive device use is a multifaceted issue with far-reaching consequences for health and society. The link between sedentary behavior and obesity underscores the urgent need for proactive measures to counteract the negative effects of digital overload. By understanding the mechanisms behind this relationship and implementing strategies to promote physical activity and mindful device use, we can pave the way for a healthier, more balanced future in the digital age.

Introduction

In an era dominated by digital technology, the pervasive use of smartphones, tablets, and computers has revolutionized the way we communicate, work, and interact. However, this digital revolution has come with its own set of health challenges, with one of the most pressing being Repetitive Strain Injuries (RSIs). These injuries, often caused by excessive typing and swiping, can have significant physical and psychological implications. In this article, we delve into the world of RSIs, exploring their causes, effects, and most importantly, how individuals can navigate the risks of excessive digital device usage.

The Rise of Digital Dependency

The rapid integration of digital devices into our daily lives has brought unprecedented convenience and connectivity. From virtual meetings to online shopping, our reliance on technology has grown exponentially. However, this digital dependency comes with a hidden cost: the increased risk of RSIs.

Understanding Repetitive Strain Injuries

1. What are RSIs?

Repetitive Strain Injuries, often referred to as RSIs or overuse injuries, encompass a range of conditions affecting the muscles, tendons, and nerves. These injuries develop gradually over time and are typically caused by repetitive and prolonged motions, such as typing, swiping, and clicking. Common examples of RSIs include *carpal tunnel syndrome* (a condition characterized by numbness, tingling, and weakness in the hand and fingers due to compression of the median nerve as it passes through the wrist's carpal tunnel), *tennis elbow* (a painful condition caused by inflammation of the tendons that attach to the outer part of the elbow, often due to overuse or repetitive motions of the forearm muscles), and *digital eyestrain* (a group of symptoms such as eye discomfort, dryness, fatigue, and blurred vision that result from prolonged use of digital devices like computers, smartphones, and tablets).

2. The Mechanics of RSIs

RSIs occur due to the strain placed on specific parts of the body through repetitive movements. When we engage in actions like typing or swiping, the same muscles and tendons are repeatedly used, leading to micro-tears, inflammation, and eventual damage. The constant pressure on these structures can impede blood flow and cause compression of nerves, resulting in pain, numbness, and reduced functionality.

The Digital Culprits: Typing and Swiping

1. The Keyboard Conundrum

Typing has become an integral part of modern work and communication. The prevalence of computer usage has led to prolonged periods of typing, which can significantly increase the risk of RSIs. The repetitive flexion and extension of the fingers and wrists can strain the tendons and muscles, leading to conditions like carpal tunnel syndrome and *tendonitis* (the inflammation or irritation of a tendon, the fibrous tissue that attaches muscles to bones, often caused by repetitive movement, overuse, or injury).

2. The Swiping Syndrome

The rise of touch-screen devices, particularly smartphones and tablets, has introduced a new type of digital danger: swiping. While swiping motions may seem less taxing compared to typing, the constant movement of the fingers and thumbs over the screen can still contribute to RSIs. Conditions like "texting thumb" and "swipe wrist" have emerged as a result of the repetitive swiping actions performed during texting, scrolling, and gaming.

The Silent Symptoms

1. Recognizing the Warning Signs

RSIs often start with subtle symptoms that are easy to dismiss. Early signs may include occasional discomfort, mild pain, or a tingling sensation. These symptoms are frequently overlooked or attributed to temporary strain. However, ignoring these warning signs can lead to more severe and persistent issues.

2. From Discomfort to Disability

If left unchecked, RSIs can progress from occasional discomfort to chronic pain and disability. Carpal tunnel syndrome, for instance, can cause numbness and weakness in the hand, making it difficult to grasp objects or perform simple tasks. Tendinitis can lead to excruciating pain and limit the range of motion in affected joints. These conditions not only impact physical well-being but can also take a toll on mental health and overall quality of life.

Prevention and Management

1. Ergonomics

Creating an ergonomic workspace is crucial for preventing RSIs. Proper positioning of the computer, keyboard, and mouse can minimize strain on the wrists, shoulders, and neck. Adjustable chairs, ergonomic keyboards, and wrist rests can provide much-needed support during extended typing sessions.

2. Taking Breaks

Frequent breaks are essential for preventing RSIs. Incorporating micro-breaks into your routine allows your muscles and tendons to recover from repetitive motions. Simple stretches and exercises can improve circulation and flexibility, reducing the risk of injury.

3. Mindful Movement

Engaging in regular exercise and stretching routines can significantly contribute to RSI prevention. Strength training and flexibility exercises help build resilient muscles and tendons, while targeted stretches can alleviate tension and improve blood flow to vulnerable areas.

4. Digital Discipline

Practicing digital discipline involves setting limits on device usage to avoid prolonged periods of typing and swiping. Utilizing productivity techniques, such as the *Pomodoro Technique* (a time management method that involves breaking work or tasks into focused intervals, typically 25 minutes in duration, followed by a short break), can help you work in focused bursts and take regular breaks.

If symptoms persist or worsen, seeking medical attention is crucial. Healthcare professionals, such as orthopedists, physical therapists, and occupational therapists, specialize in diagnosing and treating RSIs. Early intervention can prevent the progression of injuries and facilitate a faster recovery.

Conclusion

In an increasingly digitized world, the risks of repetitive strain injuries resulting from excessive typing and swiping cannot be ignored. Understanding the mechanics of RSIs, recognizing the warning signs, and adopting preventive measures are essential for maintaining our well-being in the face of digital overload. By cultivating a mindful approach to technology usage and prioritizing ergonomic practices, we can navigate the digital landscape while safeguarding our physical and mental health.

Chapter 6. The Digital Distraction Epidemic
Investigating the Impact of Gadgets on Concentration and Productivity

Introduction

In the modern era, the proliferation of digital gadgets and technologies has revolutionized the way we communicate, work, and engage with the world around us. While these advancements have brought numerous benefits, they have also ushered in a new era of challenges, one of which is the rise of digital distractions. The constant presence of smartphones, tablets, laptops, and other electronic devices has given rise to what can be aptly termed as the "digital distraction epidemic." This article delves into the profound impact of gadgets on concentration and productivity, exploring the underlying causes, consequences, and potential solutions to mitigate this growing concern.

The Pervasiveness of Digital Distractions

1. The Ubiquity of Gadgets

In the contemporary digital landscape, gadgets have become an indispensable part of daily life. People rely on their smartphones for communication, information, and entertainment, while computers and tablets have become essential tools for work and education. The portability and convenience of these devices have blurred the lines between personal and professional spheres, making it increasingly difficult to disconnect.

2. The Multitude of Distraction Sources

Digital distractions can arise from various sources, such as social media notifications, instant messaging apps, emails, and online entertainment platforms. The constant stream of information and entertainment vying for our attention has led to a phenomenon known as "continuous partial attention," where individuals find it challenging to fully engage in any single task.

The Cognitive Impact of Digital Distractions

1. The Myth of Multitasking

Contrary to popular belief, the human brain is not wired for efficient multitasking. The attempt to juggle multiple tasks simultaneously often leads to reduced cognitive performance and increased errors. Gadgets, with their multitude of distractions, exacerbate this issue by encouraging users to switch between tasks rapidly, impeding deep cognitive processing.

2. The Erosion of Attention Span

The rise of gadgets has coincided with a decline in average attention spans. Constant exposure to bite-sized content and rapid information consumption has trained our brains to seek novelty and instant gratification. As a result, individuals find it challenging to sustain focus on complex tasks that require prolonged attention and mental effort.

The Productivity Paradox

1. The Illusion of Productivity

Gadgets and digital tools are often marketed as enhancers of productivity, promising efficiency gains and streamlined workflows. However, the reality is more complex. While these tools can facilitate certain tasks, they also introduce a paradoxical dynamic where increased connectivity leads to decreased output. The constant interruptions caused by digital distractions disrupt the flow state necessary for deep work and hinder the accomplishment of meaningful tasks.

2. The Toll on Task Performance

Research has shown that frequent gadget use can significantly impair task performance. A study conducted by the University of California, Irvine, revealed that it takes an average of 23 minutes and 15 seconds to regain focus after being interrupted by a digital notification. These interruptions not only prolong task completion times but also contribute to a decline in the overall quality of work.

The Psychological Consequences

1. The Anxiety of Constant Connectivity

The "always-on" culture fostered by gadgets can lead to heightened anxiety and stress. The fear of missing out (FOMO) drives individuals to remain tethered to their devices, resulting in a continuous state of alertness. This state of hyper-vigilance can have detrimental effects on mental well-being, contributing to burnout and a sense of overwhelm.

2. The Dopamine Loop

Gadgets are designed to trigger pleasurable responses in the brain through notifications, likes, and messages. These interactions stimulate the release of dopamine, a neurotransmitter associated with reward and pleasure. The repeated exposure to this dopamine loop can lead to addictive behaviors, as individuals compulsively seek out the next digital "reward."

Mitigating the Digital Distraction Epidemic

1. Cultivating Digital Mindfulness

Mindfulness practices can play a pivotal role in combating the negative effects of digital distractions. By fostering awareness of one's digital consumption habits, individuals can make conscious choices about when and how they engage with gadgets. Techniques such as setting designated device-free periods, using notification management apps, and practicing meditation can contribute to a healthier relationship with technology.

2. Designing for Focus

The responsibility of mitigating digital distractions also falls on technology creators. User-centric design principles can help create digital environments that prioritize focus and productivity. Features such as "Do Not Disturb" modes, customizable notifications, and intelligent scheduling can empower users to regain control over their attention and time.

Conclusion

The digital distraction epidemic presents a multifaceted challenge that requires a collective effort from individuals, technology creators, and society at large. While gadgets have undeniably transformed the way we live and work, their unchecked proliferation has come at a cost to our concentration and productivity. By recognizing the cognitive and psychological impacts of digital distractions, and implementing mindful practices and thoughtful design solutions, we can navigate the digital landscape more intentionally and reclaim our ability to engage deeply with the tasks and experiences that matter most. The journey towards a balanced and focused digital existence is both a personal and societal endeavor, and its success holds the promise of a more mindful, productive, and fulfilling future.

Chapter 7. From FOMO to Digital Burnout
Analyzing the Mental Toll of Constant Connectivity

Introduction

In today's hyper-connected world, the pervasive influence of digital technology has transformed the way we live, work, and interact. While these advancements offer numerous benefits and conveniences, they also come with a darker side that often goes unnoticed - the impact of constant connectivity on our mental well-being. This article aims to delve into the evolving landscape of digital overload, exploring the journey from the Fear of Missing Out (FOMO) to the debilitating state of digital burnout, and the implications this phenomenon has for individual health and society as a whole.

The Rise of FOMO

In an era where smartphones are an extension of our bodies and social media platforms serve as digital town squares, the Fear of Missing Out (FOMO) has emerged as a widespread psychological phenomenon. FOMO, a term coined to describe the anxiety-driven sensation of being left out or missing something significant, thrives on the constant barrage of updates and notifications that flood our digital spaces. This section will explore:

1. FOMO and Social Media: FOMO and social media have intertwined to create a cycle where people fear missing out on captivating experiences shared online, while the constant pursuit of such experiences feeds the dopamine-driven loop of anticipation and reward. This dynamic keeps

users engaged on platforms like Facebook and Instagram, where curated content amplifies feelings of missing out and fuels the need for constant connection.

2. The Neurochemistry of FOMO: **FOMO** triggers intricate brain responses, involving the limbic system and stress hormones, leading to heightened emotional arousal and anxiety. The *amygdala* (a small, almond-shaped cluster of nuclei in the brain that plays a key role in processing emotions, particularly fear and other strong emotional responses) evaluates potential rewards and threats, releasing *cortisol* (a steroid hormone produced by the adrenal glands in response to stress) under FOMO's influence, while the *prefrontal cortex* (the foremost part of the brain's frontal lobe, responsible for higher cognitive functions) struggles to manage impulsive behaviors sparked by FOMO-triggering stimuli. These neural reactions illuminate how FOMO influences decision-making and emotional states.

3. Impacts on Mental Health: **FOMO's** connection to social media cultivates a distorted self-perception as users compare their lives to embellished online portrayals, fostering feelings of inadequacy, envy, and low self-esteem. The consequent pursuit of social validation intensifies anxiety, disrupts sleep patterns, and contributes to stress. Over time, these factors can escalate into more severe mental health challenges, underscoring the crucial role of FOMO in shaping digital behaviors, which may lead to social isolation and dependency on digital platforms, emphasizing the necessity of mindful engagement for a balanced and healthy relationship with technology.

The Spectrum of Digital Overload

While FOMO may serve as a gateway to digital overload, the pervasive nature of constant connectivity can push individuals into more profound states of mental distress.

1. Digital Overload Defined: Digital overload encapsulates the overwhelming sense of being inundated by a constant influx of digital information and interactions, stretching beyond the borders of FOMO. While FOMO drives a fear of missing out on captivating experiences, digital overload encompasses a broader spectrum of challenges arising from excessive digital engagement. It includes sensory overload from notifications, the constant demand for immediate responsiveness, and the compulsion to stay connected at all times.

Digital overload reflects the strain on cognitive, emotional, and social capacities as individuals grapple with maintaining an online presence, managing notifications, and consuming copious amounts of digital content. The term recognizes that the modern digital landscape extends well beyond FOMO and underscores the multifaceted pressures that individuals face in today's hyperconnected world.

2. The Cognitive Load Paradox: The cognitive load paradox elucidates the ironic consequence of information overload – as digital technologies aim to enhance convenience and knowledge-sharing, they also inundate individuals with excessive information, thereby burdening cognitive processes. The human brain has a finite capacity for processing information, and the incessant flow of data can lead to diminished attention spans, reduced ability to focus on tasks, and impaired decision-making.

The sheer volume of information, often fragmented and lacking context, challenges the brain's ability to synthesize and retain knowledge effectively. Paradoxically, while technology offers rapid access to information, it can hinder deep learning and critical thinking, straining cognitive resources and potentially leading to mental fatigue.

3. Workplace Pressures: The advent of 24/7 connectivity has significantly transformed the modern work landscape, introducing new complexities to the interplay between professional and personal life. The permeation of digital tools has eroded the boundaries between work and leisure, leading to an 'always-on' culture where work-related communication extends well beyond traditional office hours. This constant connectivity can exacerbate workplace stress, as employees find it challenging to disengage and recharge.

The pressure to respond promptly to emails, messages, and notifications blurs the lines between work and personal time, potentially leading to burnout, reduced job satisfaction, and decreased overall well-being. Furthermore, the expectation of immediate responsiveness may undermine the quality of work, as the cognitive resources required to juggle multiple tasks and communications strain individual effectiveness and creativity. The workplace pressures stemming from digital overload emphasize the need for strategies that balance technological integration with the preservation of mental health and work-life equilibrium.

Enter Digital Burnout

As digital overload intensifies, the journey from FOMO to a more debilitating state of digital burnout becomes increasingly probable. Digital burnout is characterized by exhaustion, detachment, and a sense of detachment that stems from an incessant connectivity.

1. Symptoms and Indicators: Digital burnout manifests through a range of symptoms that mirror traditional burnout but are uniquely linked to excessive digital engagement. Emotional exhaustion becomes apparent as individuals feel drained, overwhelmed, and emotionally detached due to the incessant demands of digital interactions. Decreased performance emerges as a decline in productivity, concentration, and problem-solving abilities, stemming from cognitive fatigue induced by information overload.

Cynicism, often directed towards technology or digital platforms, surfaces as a defense mechanism against the relentless digital onslaught. Additional signs may include disrupted sleep patterns, irritability, and a sense of isolation as individuals become increasingly absorbed in their digital worlds. These symptoms collectively underline the intricate relationship between technology and mental well-being, emphasizing the need for proactive interventions to mitigate digital burnout's detrimental effects.

2. Technology's Role: The design of modern digital technologies plays a pivotal role in fostering digital burnout. User interfaces engineered for maximal engagement utilize features like infinite scrolling, auto-play, and personalized recommendations, creating an addictive loop that keeps users glued to their screens. Notifications further exacerbate the problem by creating a constant state of alertness and interrupting tasks, disrupting cognitive flow.

The allure of instant gratification tied to likes, shares, and notifications stimulates the release of dopamine, reinforcing compulsive digital behaviors. This symbiotic relationship between technology design, addictive features, and notifications fuels a cycle of overstimulation, leading to cognitive fatigue and emotional strain, thereby laying the foundation for digital burnout.

3. Psychosocial Impact: Digital burnout extends beyond individual experiences to exert a substantial psychosocial toll. The excessive time spent on screens can erode the quality of face-to-face interactions, leading to a decline in genuine social connections and empathy. Virtual interactions may replace authentic communication, leading to misinterpretations and strained relationships.

Moreover, the pervasive nature of digital burnout can exacerbate feelings of loneliness and isolation, as individuals become absorbed in their devices, neglecting real-world connections. This erosion of interpersonal relationships coupled with the emotional toll of burnout can contribute to heightened stress, anxiety, and depression, underscoring the profound psychosocial impact of digital burnout on overall mental health and well-being. Addressing these challenges necessitates a holistic approach that balances technological integration with mindful digital usage and meaningful real-world interactions.

Navigating Towards Digital Well-being

While the digital landscape can pose significant challenges to mental health, it also holds the potential for positive change. This section will explore practical strategies to mitigate the adverse effects of constant connectivity and promote digital well-being, including:

1. Digital Detoxification: Digital detoxification offers a valuable reprieve from the constant onslaught of digital

stimuli, enabling individuals to reset and recharge. By intentionally disconnecting from devices and platforms, individuals can reclaim uninterrupted time for activities that promote well-being, such as spending quality time with loved ones, engaging in hobbies, or simply enjoying nature. Detox periods allow the mind to recalibrate, reducing cognitive fatigue and emotional strain caused by digital overload. These breaks offer an opportunity for reflection, fostering a renewed sense of clarity and perspective. By periodically stepping away from screens, individuals can strike a balance between their digital and real-world lives, promoting mental health and enhancing overall life satisfaction.

2. Mindful Technology Use: Mindful technology use involves a deliberate and purposeful approach to engaging with digital devices and platforms. By being present and fully engaged during digital interactions, individuals can reduce the automatic, reactive behaviors that often contribute to stress and cognitive overload. Mindfulness practices, such as setting specific intentions for technology use and periodically checking in with one's emotional state, allow for better self-regulation and awareness. Mindful engagement encourages individuals to prioritize meaningful connections and purposeful online activities while avoiding mindless scrolling or excessive consumption. Through this intentional approach, individuals can harness the benefits of technology while mitigating its potential negative impact on mental well-being.

3. Establishing Boundaries: Setting clear boundaries between work, leisure, and personal time is essential for maintaining a healthy relationship with digital devices. Establishing designated periods for checking emails or engaging in work-related tasks prevents the blurring of

professional and personal spheres, reducing work-related stress and burnout. Creating tech-free zones or designated times for digital engagement within the home environment helps preserve meaningful face-to-face interactions and fosters genuine connections. Self-regulation involves recognizing the urge to constantly check devices and consciously redirecting attention towards more fulfilling activities. By taking control of one's digital interactions, individuals can regain autonomy over their time, reduce the risk of digital burnout, and cultivate a more balanced and enriching lifestyle.

4. Promoting Digital Literacy: Digital literacy plays a pivotal role in empowering individuals to make informed choices about their online activities. Education initiatives that focus on digital literacy provide individuals with the skills to critically evaluate the credibility of online information, navigate privacy settings, and identify potential risks associated with excessive digital engagement. By promoting a better understanding of digital behaviors, individuals can develop a heightened awareness of the potential impact of their online activities on mental health. Digital literacy empowers individuals to make conscious decisions about when, where, and how they engage with technology, fostering responsible and mindful digital usage that supports their overall well-being.

Societal Implications

The effects of constant connectivity extend beyond individual well-being, shaping societal norms and values.

1. The Attention Economy: The attention economy, a driving force behind digital platforms, centers on capturing users' time and focus to generate profit through advertising and engagement. In this model, platforms compete for

attention by employing algorithms that prioritize sensational and emotionally charged content, potentially eroding attention spans and diminishing the capacity for sustained focus. The constant stream of bite-sized information can undermine critical thinking as users become accustomed to skimming content rather than delving deeply into complex subjects. Furthermore, the attention economy's emphasis on engagement over accuracy can compromise the quality of public discourse, as sensationalism and polarization are prioritized to maximize clicks and views. As digital platforms shape information consumption patterns, addressing these challenges necessitates cultivating mindfulness in consuming content and promoting platforms that prioritize informative, balanced, and well-researched discourse.

2. Privacy and Surveillance Concerns: The advent of constant connectivity has triggered profound privacy and surveillance concerns. Users' personal data is collected, analyzed, and monetized by digital platforms, raising apprehensions about data security, manipulation, and the potential for surveillance capitalism. The exchange of personal information for access to services often blurs the lines between consent and exploitation, with users inadvertently surrendering vast amounts of private data. This data can be exploited for targeted advertising, shaping individuals' beliefs and preferences. The surveillance of online behavior poses ethical questions about the balance between convenience and autonomy, underscoring the need for robust regulations to safeguard individuals' digital rights and promote transparent data practices.

3. Generational Differences: Constant connectivity has sparked generational shifts in how different age groups interact with technology and each other. Younger generations, who have grown up with digital devices,

exhibit fluidity in adapting to rapid technological changes, leveraging connectivity for communication, education, and activism. In contrast, older generations may experience challenges in navigating new technologies and coping with the pace of change. This digital divide can lead to misunderstandings and intergenerational tensions. Technology has also influenced cultural norms, shaping communication styles and social interactions. While digital natives embrace online socializing and remote work, some traditional social norms and face-to-face interactions may be altered. Understanding and bridging these generational differences in technology usage is essential for fostering meaningful connections and harnessing technology's potential to facilitate positive cultural shifts.

Conclusion

As we navigate the intricate landscape of the digital age, it is imperative to recognize and address the mental toll of constant connectivity. From the initial pangs of FOMO to the more profound state of digital burnout, understanding the trajectory of digital overload is essential for safeguarding individual well-being and shaping a more balanced relationship with technology. By embracing mindful technology use, fostering digital literacy, and advocating for changes in societal norms, we can pave the way for a healthier, more harmonious coexistence with the digital realm.

Chapter 8. Escapism and Mental Well-being
Understanding the Fine Line Between Healthy Recreation and Excessive Screen Time

Introduction

In today's fast-paced and interconnected world, the pervasiveness of digital technology has revolutionized the way we live, work, and entertain ourselves. While digital tools and platforms have undoubtedly brought numerous benefits, they have also given rise to concerns about their potential impact on mental well-being. One prominent aspect of this concern is the concept of escapism - the tendency to seek relief from everyday life's stresses and challenges through immersive digital experiences. This article delves into the intricate relationship between escapism, mental well-being, and excessive screen time, shedding light on the fine line that separates healthy recreation from potentially harmful habits.

The allure of escapism has been a part of human culture for centuries, with various forms of entertainment, literature, and art serving as vehicles for temporary reprieve from the demands of reality. In today's context, digital technology offers a diverse array of avenues for escapism, ranging from video games and social media to streaming platforms and virtual reality. As individuals increasingly turn to these digital realms, it becomes imperative to explore the impact of such behavior on mental well-being.

Escapism

1. The Nature of Escapism

Escapism is rooted in the human desire for distraction, novelty, and emotional release. It provides a temporary mental retreat from the complexities and stressors of daily life, allowing individuals to recharge and experience a sense of detachment from their problems. However, it is crucial to recognize that escapism, while beneficial in moderation, can become problematic when it evolves into excessive screen time.

2. Healthy Escapism vs. Excessive Screen Time

Healthy escapism involves engaging in recreational activities that provide relaxation and enjoyment without overshadowing other essential aspects of life. It promotes a balanced approach to digital consumption, wherein individuals are aware of their limits and engage in screen-related activities mindfully. On the other hand, excessive screen time entails an overindulgence in digital experiences, often leading to neglect of responsibilities, social isolation, and negative impacts on mental and physical health.

The Impact on Mental Well-being

1. A Positive Effects of Healthy Escapism

When harnessed in moderation, healthy escapism can contribute positively to mental well-being. Engaging in enjoyable digital activities can serve as a stress-relief mechanism, enhancing mood and reducing feelings of anxiety and depression. For example, casual gaming or watching a favorite show can provide a healthy escape from daily pressures, fostering a sense of happiness and satisfaction.

2. The Dark Side of Excessive Screen Time

Excessive screen time, however, has been linked to a range of mental health issues. Prolonged exposure to digital screens can disrupt sleep patterns, leading to insomnia and fatigue. Additionally, excessive digital engagement can contribute to feelings of social isolation and loneliness, as individuals prioritize online interactions over face-to-face relationships. The constant influx of information and virtual stimuli can overwhelm the brain, leading to cognitive overload and decreased attention span.

The Role of Dopamine

1. Dopamine's Influence on Escapism

A significant factor underlying the appeal of digital escapism is the release of dopamine - a neurotransmitter associated with pleasure and reward. Activities such as scrolling through social media feeds or achieving milestones in a video game trigger dopamine release, creating a cycle of positive reinforcement. This neurological response can encourage individuals to seek out digital experiences repeatedly, potentially leading to excessive screen time.

2. The Dopamine Dilemma

While dopamine-driven escapism can offer immediate gratification, it is essential to recognize its potential pitfalls. Relying on constant dopamine hits from digital activities can hinder an individual's ability to cope with real-world challenges and emotions. Moreover, the pursuit of short-term pleasure may impede the development of meaningful, lasting sources of happiness and fulfillment.

Finding Balance and Nurturing Well-being

1. Mindful Consumption

Achieving a healthy balance between escapism and screen time requires a conscious and mindful approach to digital consumption. Setting clear boundaries for screen use, designating tech-free times, and engaging in a variety of offline activities can help individuals cultivate a more holistic and well-rounded lifestyle.

2. Cultivating Real-world Connections

Prioritizing face-to-face interactions and nurturing genuine relationships are crucial components of mental well-being. While digital platforms offer opportunities for connection, they should complement, not replace, meaningful personal interactions.

3. Seeking Professional Support

For those struggling with the negative effects of excessive screen time, seeking professional help is essential. Mental health professionals can provide guidance on managing screen-related habits, developing coping strategies, and addressing underlying emotional issues.

Conclusion

The concept of escapism in the digital age raises significant questions about the delicate balance between healthy recreation and excessive screen time. While indulging in digital experiences can offer temporary relief from the stresses of modern life, it is crucial to approach escapism mindfully and be aware of its potential impact on mental well-being. By understanding the role of escapism, dopamine, and the importance of balance, individuals can navigate the digital landscape more consciously, fostering a healthier relationship with technology and ultimately nurturing their overall mental health and well-being.

Chapter 9. Social Media and Self-Esteem
Unpacking the Complex Relationship Between Online Validation and Identity

Introduction

The advent of the digital age has brought about a profound transformation in the way we communicate, interact, and express ourselves. Social media platforms, in particular, have become ubiquitous tools for connecting with others, sharing experiences, and forming virtual communities. However, as the digital landscape continues to evolve, concerns have emerged regarding its impact on our mental well-being and self-esteem. This article delves into the intricate interplay between social media, self-esteem, and identity, exploring how online validation influences our sense of self and contributes to the larger discourse on the impact of digital overload on health and society.

The Allure of Online Validation

1. A World of Likes and Hearts

In the era of social media, the act of receiving likes, hearts, and other forms of online validation has become a powerful psychological currency. The instant gratification of seeing notifications light up our screens can trigger a rush of positive emotions, providing a sense of affirmation and belonging. The seemingly innocuous act of double-tapping an image or clicking the "like" button has transcended into a complex mechanism through which individuals seek external validation.

Social media platforms often serve as curated showcases of our lives, presenting an idealized version of reality. The pressure to present oneself in the most favorable light can lead to a phenomenon known as the "highlight reel effect," where users predominantly share moments that are positive, glamorous, or extraordinary. This selective sharing can inadvertently create a distorted representation of reality and contribute to unrealistic societal standards. Consequently, individuals may feel compelled to continually seek online validation to uphold this façade of perfection.

The Duality of Online Validation

1. A Double-Edged Sword

While online validation can boost self-esteem and foster a sense of belonging, it can also be a double-edged sword. The ephemeral nature of digital interactions means that validation is transient and contingent upon external factors. The constant craving for validation can lead to a cycle of dependence, wherein individuals gauge their self-worth solely through online metrics. This volatile foundation for self-esteem can have adverse effects on mental health, contributing to feelings of inadequacy, anxiety, and depression.

2. The Validation Paradox

The validation paradox emerges from the disparity between the digital persona and the authentic self. As individuals strive to amass likes and followers, there is a risk of dissociation between the online identity and one's true essence. This fragmentation can lead to an existential crisis, as individuals grapple with the dissonance between the external validation they receive and their internal sense of identity.

Identity in the Digital Age

1. The Shifting Sands of Selfhood

In the digital realm, identity is no longer confined to physical attributes and geographic locations. Social media enables the construction of multifaceted identities that transcend traditional boundaries. The fluidity of online interactions allows individuals to experiment with different personas, affiliations, and communities. However, this malleability can also blur the lines between authenticity and performance, making it challenging to ascertain where the virtual self ends and the genuine self begins.

2. From Individual to Collective Identity

Social media platforms have ushered in an era of collective identity, where individuals align themselves with various online groups and communities. These digital tribes offer a sense of belonging and shared purpose, but they can also contribute to the fragmentation of individual identity. As the boundaries between the self and the collective become intertwined, individuals may find themselves navigating a complex web of allegiances, values, and expectations.

Navigating the Nexus

1. Mindful Consumption

Cultivating awareness of one's online behavior is paramount in mitigating the potential pitfalls of social media. Mindful consumption involves critically evaluating the content we consume and being attuned to its impact on our emotions and self-perception. Engaging with social media through a discerning lens can help individuals avoid the pitfalls of constant comparison and filter bubbles, promoting a more balanced relationship with online validation.

2. Authentic Storytelling

Counteracting the validation paradox necessitates a shift towards authentic storytelling. Embracing vulnerability and sharing the full spectrum of human experiences can foster genuine connections and resonate with others on a deeper level. By dismantling the façade of perfection, individuals can contribute to a more authentic online culture that celebrates imperfection and nurtures meaningful interactions.

3. Fostering Digital Resilience

Building digital resilience is essential in safeguarding one's self-esteem in the face of the unpredictable nature of online validation. This involves cultivating a strong sense of self-worth that is rooted in internal validation rather than external metrics. Developing coping strategies to manage the fluctuations of online validation can empower individuals to navigate the digital landscape with greater emotional well-being.

Conclusion

The intricate relationship between social media, self-esteem, and identity underscores the complex interplay between digital technology and human psychology. As we grapple with the impact of digital overload on health and society, it is imperative to recognize that online validation is a multifaceted phenomenon that can both elevate and erode our sense of self. By fostering mindful engagement, embracing authenticity, and nurturing digital resilience, individuals can navigate the digital age while preserving their mental well-being and cultivating a more holistic sense of identity. As we continue to evolve in the digital era, understanding and managing this complex relationship remains a pivotal aspect of our collective journey.

Chapter 10. Cyberbullying and Digital Harassment
Exploring the Dark Side of Online Interactions

Introduction

In the rapidly evolving digital age, the emergence of new communication technologies has revolutionized the way we interact, share information, and connect with others. While these advancements have undoubtedly brought about numerous benefits, they have also given rise to a darker aspect of online interactions: cyberbullying and digital harassment. As part of the book on the "Impact of Digital Overload on Health and Society," this article delves into the multifaceted dimensions of cyberbullying and digital harassment, shedding light on their detrimental effects on individuals and society at large.

Defining Cyberbullying and Digital Harassment

1. Cyberbullying

Cyberbullying refers to the act of deliberately using digital platforms, such as social media, messaging apps, and online forums, to target, threaten, harass, or intimidate another individual. Unlike traditional forms of bullying, which typically occurred in physical settings, cyberbullying exploits the anonymity and reach of the internet to inflict harm on victims. This form of aggression can take various forms, including verbal abuse, spreading rumors, sharing personal information without consent, and posting derogatory comments or images.

2. Digital Harassment

Digital harassment encompasses a broader spectrum of negative online behaviors, which extend beyond bullying to include activities such as stalking, impersonation, doxing (publishing private information with malicious intent), and sending unsolicited explicit content. This form of harassment leverages the digital landscape to violate an individual's privacy, create feelings of insecurity, and erode their online and offline well-being.

The Digital Playground

1. Anonymity

The internet's anonymity feature allows users to conceal their identities, providing a breeding ground for cyberbullies to operate without accountability. Perpetrators can mask their true selves and carry out harmful actions with minimal fear of consequences, making it challenging to pinpoint and confront them.

2. Digital Disinhibition

Psychological studies have revealed the concept of "online disinhibition effect," where individuals tend to display more aggressive and impulsive behavior online due to a perceived sense of detachment from real-world consequences. This phenomenon further exacerbates the prevalence of cyberbullying, as individuals feel empowered to unleash their negative emotions and engage in harmful actions they might refrain from in face-to-face interactions.

Impacts on Individuals

1. Emotional and Psychological Toll

Cyberbullying and digital harassment can inflict severe emotional and psychological wounds on victims. The constant barrage of hurtful messages and derogatory content can lead to anxiety, depression, and low self-esteem. Victims may feel isolated and helpless, struggling to escape the digital onslaught that follows them everywhere.

2. Physical Consequences

The distress caused by online harassment can manifest physically, leading to sleep disturbances, headaches, and even exacerbating pre-existing health conditions. The relentless stress imposed by cyberbullying may also compromise the immune system, leaving victims vulnerable to various illnesses.

Societal Ramifications

1. Undermining Social Fabric

As the digital sphere intertwines with the physical world, cyberbullying's impact extends beyond individual victims. Communities and societies at large face the risk of social cohesion erosion, as the anonymity of the online environment can encourage callousness and indifference towards others' suffering. This can weaken the bonds that hold societies together, fostering an environment of mistrust and isolation.

2. Generational Divide

The younger generation, being more immersed in the digital realm, is particularly susceptible to the effects of cyberbullying. Long-lasting emotional scars can disrupt adolescents' healthy development, hindering their ability to form meaningful relationships and achieve their full potential.

Addressing the Crisis

1. Education and Awareness

Raising awareness about the consequences of cyberbullying is paramount in combatting this digital menace. Educational institutions, parents, and online platforms must collaborate to impart knowledge and promote responsible online behavior. Teaching digital etiquette and empathy can empower individuals to foster a safer online environment.

2. Legal and Policy Measures

Governments and legal authorities worldwide are recognizing the urgency of addressing cyberbullying through legislation. Enacting and enforcing laws that hold perpetrators accountable for their online actions can act as a deterrent and provide justice to victims. Furthermore, platforms should establish clear guidelines and reporting mechanisms to swiftly address instances of harassment.

3. Promoting Digital Resilience

Digital resilience entails equipping individuals with the emotional tools to navigate the online world's challenges. Developing coping strategies, building self-confidence, and encouraging open communication can help individuals withstand cyberbullying and emerge stronger from its clutches.

Conclusion

The digital age has brought about remarkable advancements that shape the way we communicate and interact. However, the shadow of cyberbullying and digital harassment reminds us of the perilous consequences of unchecked online aggression. As we strive to strike a balance between technological progress and societal well-being, it is imperative that we collectively address the dark side of online interactions, ensuring a safer and healthier digital landscape for generations to come.

Introduction

In the 21st century, the rise of digital technology has transformed nearly every aspect of our lives, including how we parent our children. While these advancements have brought numerous benefits, they have also ushered in a new era of challenges for parents. As gadgets become increasingly integrated into our daily routines, it is crucial to examine their impact on children's development and relationships. This article delves into the complex landscape of digital parenting, shedding light on the multifaceted challenges that parents face in nurturing healthy growth and meaningful connections in the digital age.

The Digital Landscape

1. Advantages of Digital Engagement

Digital gadgets, such as smartphones, tablets, and computers, offer a myriad of opportunities for learning, creativity, and entertainment. Educational apps, interactive games, and online resources can enhance cognitive development, critical thinking, and problem-solving skills. Additionally, digital connectivity allows children to explore diverse cultures, perspectives, and global issues, promoting a broader worldview from a young age.

2. Perils of Excessive Screen Time

On the flip side, excessive screen time has raised concerns about its impact on physical and mental health. Prolonged exposure to screens has been linked to sedentary behavior, disrupted sleep patterns, and even vision problems. Moreover, a growing body of research suggests a potential correlation between excessive screen time and developmental issues, including attention deficits and impaired social skills.

The Parental Balancing Act

1. Establishing Healthy Boundaries

Digital parenting entails striking a delicate balance between leveraging the benefits of technology and safeguarding children from its potential pitfalls. One of the primary challenges parents face is setting appropriate limits on screen time. Establishing consistent routines, designating screen-free zones, and employing parental control apps can help mitigate the risks of excessive gadget use.

2. Modeling Healthy Behavior

Parents play a pivotal role in shaping their children's relationship with technology. By modeling responsible gadget usage, parents can impart valuable lessons on self-discipline, time management, and prioritizing real-world interactions. Engaging in joint activities, such as outdoor play, board games, and family outings, fosters quality time and reinforces the importance of balanced living.

Impact on Cognitive Development and Learning

1. Digital Learning Tools

The digital landscape offers a wealth of learning opportunities through interactive platforms, virtual simulations, and online courses. These tools can enhance children's engagement with educational content and facilitate personalized learning experiences. Moreover, digital resources can cater to diverse learning styles, enabling children to grasp complex concepts in innovative ways.

2. Cognitive Challenges and Digital Distractions

However, the constant influx of information and stimuli from gadgets can lead to cognitive challenges. Rapid task-switching and frequent interruptions can hinder sustained attention and hinder deep learning. The instant gratification provided by digital devices may discourage patience and perseverance in tackling more demanding intellectual pursuits.

Navigating Social and Emotional Development

1. Virtual vs. Face-to-Face Interaction

Digital technology has redefined how children interact with peers and form social connections. While online platforms enable global communication and networking, they can also impact the development of essential interpersonal skills. Virtual interactions, devoid of nonverbal cues, may hinder children's ability to interpret emotions and build empathy, potentially affecting the quality of their relationships.

The digital realm exposes children to risks such as cyberbullying, online predators, and inappropriate content. Parents must equip their children with the necessary skills to navigate these challenges safely. Open communication, digital literacy education, and establishing trust-based relationships empower children to make informed choices and seek assistance when faced with online threats.

Fostering Creativity Amidst Digital Distractions

1. Digital Creativity and Expression

Digital gadgets provide a platform for children to express their creativity through art, music, writing, and multimedia projects. Apps and software designed for artistic endeavors can spark innovation and allow children to experiment with various forms of self-expression.

2. Unplugged Creativity

Balancing digital and analog experiences is crucial for nurturing holistic creativity. Encouraging children to engage in offline activities, such as hands-on crafts, imaginative play, and outdoor exploration, promotes divergent thinking and helps them develop a well-rounded creative skill set.

Conclusion

The digital age has redefined the landscape of parenting, presenting both opportunities and challenges. While gadgets offer immense potential for learning, creativity, and connectivity, parents must be vigilant in mitigating the negative effects of excessive screen time on children's development. Striking a harmonious balance between digital engagement and offline experiences is essential for fostering healthy cognitive, social, and emotional growth. As we navigate the complexities of digital parenting, it is crucial to remain adaptable, well-informed, and committed to nurturing a generation that thrives in the digital world while maintaining meaningful connections in the real one.

Chapter 12. The Erosion of Face-to-Face Communication
Assessing How Gadgets Affect Interpersonal Relationships

Introduction

In the digital age, gadgets have become ubiquitous, seamlessly integrating into every facet of our lives. These devices have undoubtedly revolutionized the way we communicate and access information. However, their pervasive presence has also sparked concerns about the erosion of face-to-face communication and its impact on interpersonal relationships. This article delves into the complex interplay between gadgets and interpersonal interactions, highlighting both the benefits and drawbacks of this evolving landscape.

The Rise of Gadgets and Digital Communication

1. A Technological Revolution

The past few decades have witnessed an unparalleled technological revolution, marked by the advent of smartphones, tablets, and laptops. These gadgets have enabled us to stay connected with a simple tap, regardless of geographical boundaries. The convenience and speed of digital communication have reshaped our expectations of interaction, emphasizing instant gratification.

2. Convenience at Our Fingertips

Gadgets have streamlined our lives, making tasks like sending messages, making calls, and sharing media effortless. Social media platforms and messaging apps have become extensions of our social circles, enabling us to maintain connections with friends and family, regardless of physical distance. Virtual interactions have become second nature, blurring the lines between online and offline relationships.

The Paradox of Connectivity

1. The Illusion of Connection

While gadgets promise connectivity, there is a growing concern that they may be fostering a sense of isolation. The paradox lies in the fact that despite being digitally connected, individuals may experience a decline in meaningful face-to-face interactions. Virtual communication often lacks the depth and nuance of in-person conversations, potentially hindering the development of authentic relationships.

2. The Diminishing Art of Conversation

Face-to-face communication offers the advantage of nonverbal cues, such as facial expressions and body language, which are vital for understanding emotions and building rapport. Gadgets, however, limit the expression of these cues, leading to misinterpretation and emotional detachment. As a result, the art of conversation is at risk of erosion, as individuals become accustomed to asynchronous and abbreviated digital interactions.

Impact on Interpersonal Relationships

1. Shifting Dynamics in Family Life

Gadgets have introduced a new dynamic within families, transforming traditional bonding activities. While they can facilitate communication when family members are apart, they can also lead to physical presence without genuine engagement. Shared moments, such as meals and outings, may be disrupted by the constant pull of digital distractions, potentially weakening family bonds.

2. Friends in the Digital Age

The concept of friendship has evolved with the rise of social media. While platforms offer the opportunity to connect with a vast network of acquaintances, they can blur the distinction between genuine friendships and casual online connections. Maintaining hundreds of virtual friendships may dilute the time and energy available for nurturing deeper, offline relationships.

3. Romantic Relationships in a Digital World

Digital gadgets have both enriched and complicated romantic relationships. Couples can stay connected throughout the day, sharing experiences and emotions in real-time. However, the allure of gadgets can also lead to excessive screen time, diverting attention from partners and eroding intimacy. The pressure to curate a perfect digital persona can create unrealistic expectations, potentially straining relationships.

Navigating the Digital Landscape Mindfully

1. Setting Boundaries

To mitigate the erosion of face-to-face communication, it is crucial to establish healthy boundaries with gadgets. Designating tech-free zones or times can provide opportunities for meaningful interactions without distractions. Families can reclaim quality time by embracing activities that promote engagement and dialogue, fostering stronger connections.

2. Fostering Digital Literacy

Promoting digital literacy is essential to navigate the digital landscape mindfully. Educating individuals, especially children and adolescents, about the potential pitfalls of excessive gadget use can empower them to make conscious choices. Developing the skills to interpret and respond to digital communication in a nuanced manner can bridge the gap between virtual and in-person interactions.

3. Embracing Hybrid Interaction

Rather than viewing gadgets as a threat to face-to-face communication, they can be leveraged to enhance interactions. Hybrid interaction involves using gadgets to facilitate meaningful in-person conversations, such as sharing photos or discussing articles. Striking a balance between virtual and physical connections can harness the strengths of both mediums while mitigating their respective drawbacks.

Conclusion

The erosion of face-to-face communication in the digital age is a multifaceted issue that warrants careful consideration. Gadgets have undoubtedly transformed the way we connect, bridging geographical gaps and enabling instantaneous communication. However, the allure of constant connectivity can come at the cost of meaningful interpersonal relationships. By navigating the digital landscape mindfully, setting boundaries, and fostering digital literacy, we can strike a harmonious balance between the convenience of gadgets and the depth of face-to-face communication. As we continue to grapple with the impact of digital overload on health and society, it is imperative to prioritize and nurture the essence of genuine human connections.

Introduction

In today's fast-paced digital world, the realm of romantic relationships has undergone a significant transformation. The rise of online dating platforms and the increasing prevalence of long-distance relationships have redefined the way people connect, interact, and form emotional bonds. This article delves into the intricate dynamics of love in the digital age, focusing on the impact of online dating and long-distance relationships on individuals' emotional well-being, societal norms, and the potential challenges posed by digital overload.

The Rise of Online Dating

1. The Digital Matchmaker

The advent of online dating has revolutionized the way people approach romantic relationships. These platforms provide a virtual space where individuals can meet potential partners based on shared interests, preferences, and compatibility algorithms. The sheer convenience and accessibility of online dating have empowered individuals to expand their dating pool beyond geographical constraints, allowing for connections that might not have been possible before.

Historically, online dating carried a certain stigma, often viewed as a last resort for those unable to find love through traditional means. However, societal perceptions have evolved, and online dating is now widely accepted as a legitimate way to meet partners. This shift in attitude has paved the way for a more diverse and inclusive dating landscape.

The Dynamics of Long-Distance Relationships

1. Love Beyond Borders

Long-distance relationships (LDRs) have become increasingly common as people pursue education, career opportunities, and personal growth in different locations. The digital age has provided tools that enable couples to maintain connections despite physical separation. Video calls, messaging apps, and social media platforms offer a sense of closeness that helps bridge the gap created by distance.

2. Challenges and Benefits of Long-Distance Love

While long-distance relationships offer unique opportunities for personal growth and independence, they also present challenges. The lack of physical proximity can lead to feelings of loneliness, jealousy, and insecurity. However, couples who successfully navigate the challenges of LDRs often report stronger emotional bonds and effective communication skills, factors that can contribute to long-term relationship success.

The Impact on Emotional Well-Being

1. The Paradox of Choice and Decision Fatigue

The vast array of potential partners available through online dating can lead to decision fatigue, where individuals struggle to make choices due to an overwhelming number of options. While having options is empowering, it can also lead to anxiety and uncertainty, impacting emotional well-being.

2. Emotional Intimacy in the Digital Age

Digital communication tools have reshaped the landscape of emotional intimacy. Couples in long-distance relationships often rely on text messages, voice calls, and video chats to maintain a sense of closeness. These tools allow for constant connection but may also lead to a shallow sense of intimacy compared to face-to-face interactions. Striking a balance between digital and in-person interactions is crucial for fostering deep emotional connections.

Redefining Societal Norms

1. Challenging Geographical Boundaries

Online dating and long-distance relationships challenge traditional notions of geographical boundaries in relationships. The ability to connect with someone from a different city, country, or culture introduces new perspectives and experiences, enriching individuals' lives and broadening their horizons.

Digital relationships often follow a non-linear progression. Couples may spend considerable time communicating online before meeting in person, altering the traditional trajectory of relationship development. This shift challenges conventional expectations and highlights the importance of emotional connections in the early stages of a relationship.

The Threat of Digital Overload

1. The Digital Paradox

While the digital age has expanded the possibilities for connection, it has also raised concerns about the potential negative impact of excessive screen time. Digital overload, characterized by constant notifications, multitasking, and online compulsions, can strain relationships and hinder genuine emotional engagement.

2. Strategies for Balancing Digital and Emotional Realms

To mitigate the effects of digital overload, individuals in online and long-distance relationships must establish boundaries and mindful screen time practices. Creating dedicated spaces for face-to-face interactions and setting aside tech-free moments can foster more authentic connections and promote emotional well-being.

Navigating the Future of Love

1. Technological Evolution and Relationship Dynamics

As technology continues to advance, the landscape of love and relationships will inevitably evolve further. Virtual reality, augmented reality, and artificial intelligence have the potential to reshape how people connect and interact. These technologies could enhance emotional intimacy or, conversely, lead to further challenges in maintaining genuine human connections.

2. The Role of Self-Awareness and Adaptation

In the midst of the digital revolution, self-awareness and adaptability remain essential. Individuals must reflect on their emotional needs and be willing to adapt their communication styles to suit the demands of their relationships. By recognizing the potential pitfalls of the digital age and proactively addressing them, individuals can forge deeper, more meaningful connections.

Conclusion

Love in the digital age is a complex and multifaceted phenomenon, shaped by the intersection of online dating platforms, long-distance relationships, and the challenges of digital overload. As society continues to grapple with the implications of the digital revolution, individuals must navigate the delicate balance between virtual connections and genuine emotional intimacy. By fostering self-awareness, open communication, and mindful tech practices, individuals can cultivate relationships that transcend the digital realm and stand the test of time.

Chapter 14. Gadgets at the Dinner Table
Analyzing the Impact of Device Use on Family Bonds and Social Gatherings

Introduction

In today's digital age, gadgets have become an integral part of our daily lives. From smartphones to tablets and laptops, these devices have revolutionized the way we communicate, work, and entertain ourselves. However, their pervasive presence has also given rise to concerns about the impact of device use on our health and social interactions. One particularly significant arena where this impact is felt is at the dinner table. Traditionally a space for family bonding and social gatherings, the intrusion of gadgets into this sacred space has led to a shift in dynamics and raised questions about the long-term consequences on relationships and society. This article delves into the multifaceted issue of gadgets at the dinner table, analyzing their influence on family bonds and social interactions.

The Dinner Table as a Hub of Connectivity

1. Historical Significance of the Dinner Table

The dinner table has long held a crucial role in human society, serving as a nexus for family members to gather, share stories, and strengthen their bonds. Historically, meals have been a time for face-to-face interactions, fostering emotional connections and facilitating the passing down of traditions and values.

2. Digital Devices: A Modern Intrusion

The rapid integration of digital devices into our lives has led to their presence even at the dinner table. With the constant allure of notifications, social media updates, and online entertainment, individuals are increasingly finding it difficult to resist the pull of their gadgets during meals. This intrusion has the potential to disrupt the traditional dynamics of the dinner table, altering the quality and depth of interactions.

Shifting Dynamics and Erosion of Bonds

1. Diminished Face-to-Face Engagement

One of the most significant impacts of gadget use at the dinner table is the decline in face-to-face engagement. Instead of engaging in meaningful conversations with family members, individuals may find themselves engrossed in their devices, thus missing out on valuable opportunities for connection and communication.

2. Erosion of Shared Experiences

The act of sharing a meal has traditionally provided an avenue for sharing experiences, both big and small. With gadgets stealing the spotlight, the shared experience of enjoying a meal and exchanging stories can diminish, potentially leading to a loss of common ground and emotional intimacy.

Device Use and Social Gatherings

1. The Changing Landscape of Social Gatherings

Beyond family dinners, the impact of device use extends to broader social gatherings. Parties, celebrations, and group outings are all vulnerable to the intrusion of gadgets. The allure of capturing and sharing the moment on social media can sometimes overshadow the genuine enjoyment of the event.

2. Fostering Disconnect in Connected Spaces

Paradoxically, the digital devices that are supposed to connect us to a wider world can foster a sense of disconnect in social gatherings. When individuals prioritize virtual interactions over in-person ones, it can lead to superficial conversations and a lack of true engagement with others present.

Navigating a Balanced Future

1. Recognizing the Need for Change

Acknowledging the potential harm caused by excessive gadget use at the dinner table and social gatherings is the first step toward finding a solution. By understanding the value of meaningful face-to-face interactions, individuals can begin to recognize the importance of breaking away from digital distractions.

2. Establishing Healthy Boundaries

Creating and maintaining healthy boundaries around gadget use during meals and social gatherings is vital. Families and social groups can set ground rules that encourage device-free zones, allowing everyone to fully engage and connect with each other.

3. Embracing Mindful Device Use

Rather than demonizing technology, individuals can learn to embrace mindful device use. This involves consciously choosing when and how to use gadgets, ensuring that they enhance, rather than hinder, social interactions.

Conclusion

The intrusion of gadgets at the dinner table and social gatherings represents a complex challenge in our digital age. While these devices have undoubtedly brought convenience and connection, they have also posed threats to the deep bonds and meaningful interactions that traditionally occurred during meals and group events. As we navigate this evolving landscape, it is crucial to recognize the value of genuine face-to-face connections and prioritize moments of human interaction that strengthen our family bonds and societal fabric. By establishing healthy boundaries and practicing mindful device use, we can hope to strike a balance between the benefits of technology and the preservation of our essential human connections.

Chapter 15. Tech Industry's Role in Public Health
Examining Corporate Accountability and Ethical Design

Introduction

In today's hyper-connected world, the rapid advancement of technology has led to a digital revolution that has transformed almost every aspect of our lives. From communication and entertainment to healthcare and education, technology has undoubtedly brought about numerous benefits. However, as our reliance on digital devices and platforms continues to grow, concerns about the impact of digital overload on both individual health and societal well-being have also escalated. This article delves into the critical role the tech industry plays in public health, focusing on the concepts of corporate accountability and ethical design. By examining these aspects, we aim to shed light on how the tech industry can mitigate the negative consequences of digital overload and contribute to a healthier and more balanced digital ecosystem.

The Digital Overload Phenomenon

The proliferation of smartphones, social media, and various digital services has given rise to the phenomenon of digital overload. This term refers to the excessive use of digital technologies, which can lead to various health and social issues, including stress, anxiety, sleep disorders, and reduced physical activity. With people spending increasing amounts of time online, the tech industry's role in shaping the digital landscape becomes crucial.

Corporate Accountability and its Significance

As technology companies continue to develop and market digital products, they assume a significant level of responsibility for the well-being of their users. Corporate accountability in the tech industry involves recognizing the potential negative consequences of digital overload and taking active steps to address them. This accountability extends beyond mere legal compliance and encompasses ethical considerations that prioritize user health and societal welfare.

1. Data Privacy and User Protection

One key aspect of corporate accountability is safeguarding user data and privacy. Tech companies must establish robust data protection mechanisms to ensure that users' personal information remains secure. Recent data breaches and scandals have highlighted the urgent need for stringent privacy measures, compelling the tech industry to reevaluate its practices and prioritize transparency.

2. Addressing Addiction and Overuse

The addictive nature of digital platforms is a growing concern. To fulfill their corporate accountability, tech companies must acknowledge the potential for addiction and overuse in their products. Implementing features that encourage responsible usage and limit excessive screen time demonstrates a commitment to user well-being.

Ethical Design Principles for Healthier Technology

Ethical design involves creating digital products with a focus on user welfare, promoting a healthier relationship between individuals and technology. By adhering to ethical design principles, the tech industry can proactively contribute to public health and mitigate the negative effects of digital overload.

1. User-Centric Design

Putting users' needs and well-being at the forefront of product design is a fundamental ethical principle. This involves creating intuitive interfaces, minimizing distractions, and optimizing user experience to reduce stress and cognitive overload.

2. Nudging Towards Positive Behavior

Tech companies can employ behavioral nudges to encourage users to make healthier choices. For instance, incorporating features that promote breaks, physical activity, and social interactions can guide users toward more balanced digital habits.

3. Transparent Algorithms and Content Curation

Transparency in algorithmic decision-making and content curation is essential to ensure that users receive information that is accurate, diverse, and relevant. Ethical design entails providing users with insights into how algorithms work and allowing them to have greater control over their digital experience.

Collaborative Efforts

Mitigating the negative impact of digital overload requires collaborative efforts among various stakeholders. The tech industry, researchers, and regulators must work together to establish guidelines, policies, and practices that prioritize public health and societal well-being.

1. Industry-Research Partnerships

Collaboration between technology companies and researchers can lead to a better understanding of the psychological and physiological effects of digital overload. By sharing data and insights, both parties can develop effective strategies to address potential harm and promote responsible technology use.

2. Regulatory Frameworks

Governments and regulatory bodies play a vital role in ensuring that the tech industry adheres to ethical design principles and corporate accountability. Implementing and enforcing regulations that promote user well-being can create a healthier digital environment for all.

Education and Digital Literacy

Promoting digital literacy and awareness is essential to empower individuals to make informed decisions about their technology use. Education campaigns, workshops, and resources can help users develop healthy digital habits and navigate the digital landscape responsibly.

1. Media Literacy Programs

Teaching individuals how to critically evaluate digital content can enhance their ability to discern credible information from misinformation. Media literacy programs can equip users with the skills needed to navigate the vast digital landscape effectively.

Educating parents and educators about the potential risks of digital overload and providing them with tools to guide children's technology use is crucial. By instilling responsible digital habits from a young age, we can create a future generation that is more mindful of their technology consumption.

Conclusion

The tech industry's role in public health is a multifaceted endeavor that encompasses corporate accountability, ethical design, collaboration among stakeholders, and promoting digital literacy. By recognizing their responsibility and actively implementing strategies that prioritize user well-being, technology companies can contribute to a healthier and more balanced digital ecosystem. As the digital revolution continues to shape our world, it is imperative that we address the challenges of digital overload and work together to create a future where technology enhances, rather than hinders, our well-being and societal harmony.

Introduction

In the modern era, the pervasive influence of digital technology has transformed the way we interact, work, and live. While these advancements have undoubtedly brought convenience and efficiency, they have also given rise to concerns about the impact of excessive device use on individual health and societal well-being. This article delves into the realm of government policies and digital detox initiatives, exploring various strategies aimed at mitigating the adverse effects of digital overload on both physical and mental health.

The Rise of Digital Overload and its Consequences

1. The Digital Revolution's Dual Face

The digital revolution has ushered in an age of unparalleled connectivity and access to information, fundamentally altering how people communicate, learn, and entertain themselves. Simultaneously, it has led to an increase in screen time, with individuals of all ages spending substantial hours immersed in their devices, whether for work or leisure. This excessive usage has given rise to a range of adverse consequences, from sleep disturbances and eye strain to reduced physical activity and impaired social interactions.

2. The Health Implications

The implications of digital overload on health are multifaceted. Prolonged screen time has been linked to an array of health issues, including digital eye strain, disrupted circadian rhythms, and sedentary behavior. Moreover, excessive device use has been correlated with an increased risk of obesity, anxiety, depression, and other mental health disorders, particularly among the younger population. These health concerns have prompted governments and health authorities to take action.

Government Policies to Address Digital Overload

1. The Regulatory Landscape

Governments around the world have recognized the urgent need to address the challenges posed by digital overload. Regulatory measures have been introduced to safeguard public health and promote responsible technology use. These policies range from limiting screen time for children and adolescents to imposing guidelines on online advertising targeting vulnerable populations.

2. Age-Specific Regulations

Recognizing the susceptibility of children and adolescents to the adverse effects of excessive device use, many countries have implemented age-specific regulations. These measures include setting limits on screen time in schools, encouraging parental controls, and incorporating digital literacy programs into curricula to foster healthy technology habits from an early age.

3. Advertising and Content Regulations

Governments are increasingly concerned about the influence of digital advertising on consumer behavior, especially among young individuals. Stricter regulations on targeted advertising to minors and limitations on the promotion of unhealthy products have been implemented to reduce the potential harm caused by aggressive digital marketing strategies.

4. Workplace Regulations

The blurring lines between work and personal life in the digital age have prompted governments to address the impact of excessive device use on the workforce. Some countries have introduced "right to disconnect" laws, which grant employees the right to disconnect from work-related digital communications outside of working hours. These policies aim to mitigate burnout and promote a healthier work-life balance.

Digital Detox Initiatives

1. Public Awareness Campaigns

Governments and non-governmental organizations (NGOs) are collaborating to raise awareness about the consequences of digital overload and promote digital detox. Public awareness campaigns are designed to educate individuals about the importance of limiting screen time, engaging in physical activity, and nurturing face-to-face relationships.

2. Technological Interventions

Ironically, technology itself is being leveraged to combat digital overload. Digital wellness apps and features embedded within operating systems enable users to track their screen time, set usage limits, and receive notifications encouraging breaks. These interventions empower individuals to take control of their device usage and make informed decisions about their digital habits.

3. Digital-Free Zones and Retreats

In an effort to create spaces that facilitate disconnection from digital devices, some governments and private entities have established digital-free zones in public places, such as parks, libraries, and recreational centers. Additionally, digital detox retreats provide individuals with an immersive environment free from digital distractions, encouraging them to reengage with nature and cultivate mindfulness.

4. Corporate Social Responsibility

Recognizing their role in shaping digital behavior, technology companies are increasingly embracing corporate social responsibility initiatives. Some companies have introduced features that remind users to take breaks, while others support digital wellness programs in schools and communities. These initiatives reflect a growing commitment to address the negative impacts of excessive device use.

Challenges and Future Directions

1. Balancing Innovation with Responsibility

One of the main challenges in formulating effective policies and initiatives is striking a balance between technological innovation and safeguarding public health. Governments must navigate the delicate task of encouraging responsible device use without stifling technological progress and economic growth.

2. Cultural and Societal Factors

The impact of digital overload varies across cultures and societies, making it imperative for policies and initiatives to consider cultural nuances and societal norms. Strategies that are effective in one context may not necessarily translate to another, necessitating a flexible and culturally sensitive approach.

3. Research and Evaluation

The effectiveness of government policies and digital detox initiatives relies on robust research and continuous evaluation. Governments must invest in long-term studies to assess the impact of their interventions on public health, behavior, and well-being. This iterative approach ensures that strategies can be refined and adapted based on evidence-based insights.

4. Collaboration and Multi-Stakeholder Engagement

Addressing the multifaceted challenges of digital overload requires collaboration among governments, technology companies, healthcare providers, educators, and civil society organizations. Multi-stakeholder partnerships can foster innovative solutions and amplify the impact of digital detox initiatives on a global scale.

Conclusion

The proliferation of digital technology has brought about unprecedented connectivity and convenience, but it has also given rise to the perils of digital overload. Governments and stakeholders have recognized the urgency of countering excessive device use to protect individual and societal well-being. Through a combination of regulatory measures, public awareness campaigns, technological interventions, and collaborative efforts, strategies are being developed to promote responsible digital habits and mitigate the adverse effects of digital overload. As we navigate the uncharted territory of the digital age, it is essential to continue innovating and refining approaches to ensure a harmonious balance between technology and human well-being.

Chapter 17. Promoting Digital Well-being
Showcasing Successful Campaigns and Interventions

Introduction

In an era defined by unprecedented technological advancements, the pervasive influence of digital devices and platforms on our lives cannot be overstated. The rapid integration of technology into various aspects of society has led to numerous benefits, but it has also given rise to concerns about the impact of digital overload on both individual health and the broader social fabric. As the world grapples with the consequences of excessive digital engagement, a growing emphasis is being placed on promoting digital well-being. This article delves into successful campaigns and interventions that have been devised to address the challenges posed by digital overload, highlighting their impact and offering insights for a healthier digital future.

Understanding Digital Overload and its Consequences

Before delving into successful campaigns and interventions, it is crucial to establish a clear understanding of digital overload and the potential harm it can cause to individuals and society at large.

1. Defining Digital Overload

Digital overload refers to the excessive consumption of digital content and engagement with digital devices, leading to negative physical, psychological, and social outcomes. It encompasses behaviors such as constant smartphone use, compulsive social media scrolling, information overload, and digital dependency.

2. Consequences of Digital Overload

Physical Health: Prolonged screen time can lead to digital eye strain, disrupted sleep patterns, and sedentary lifestyles.

Mental Health: Excessive digital engagement has been linked to increased stress, anxiety, depression, and feelings of social isolation.

Productivity and Creativity: Overreliance on digital devices can hinder productivity and creative thinking.

Social Interactions: Excessive use of social media may lead to superficial relationships, reduced face-to-face interactions, and a distorted sense of reality.

Successful Campaigns and Interventions

Efforts to address digital overload and promote digital well-being have taken various forms, from awareness campaigns to technological solutions. The following sections highlight some noteworthy campaigns and interventions that have yielded positive results.

1. Digital Detox Campaigns

National Day of Unplugging: Initiatives like the National Day of Unplugging encourage individuals to disconnect from digital devices for a set period, promoting mindful offline activities and human connections.

Digital Sabbaticals: Companies and organizations are offering employees the option to take digital sabbaticals, allowing them to recharge and reduce digital stress. A digital sabbatical is a deliberate period of time during which individuals disconnect from digital devices and online activities to promote mental well-being and reconnect with offline experiences.

2. Mindfulness and Mental Health Apps

Headspace: This popular app offers guided meditation and mindfulness exercises to help users manage stress and develop healthier relationships with technology.

Calm: Calm provides a range of meditation and relaxation techniques, aiding users in reducing digital dependency and fostering mental well-being.

3. Design and User Experience Interventions

Digital Well-being Features: Tech giants like Apple and Google have introduced features that allow users to monitor and limit their screen time, helping them regain control over their digital usage.

Nudge Theory: Nudge theory is a concept in behavioral economics and psychology that involves using subtle, indirect suggestions (nudges) to influence people's decisions and behavior in a predictable and positive way, often without restricting their freedom of choice. Nudge theory aims to guide individuals towards making better choices by altering the context or presentation of options, making the desired choice more attractive or easier to select. It is based on the idea that small, well-designed interventions can have a significant impact on decision-making and encourage more favorable outcomes. By integrating principles of user experience design, individuals can be gently guided toward adopting healthier digital behaviors; for instance, social media platforms can promote intervals between browsing sessions to encourage mindful usage.

4. Education and Advocacy Initiatives

Digital Literacy Programs: Schools and organizations are implementing digital literacy programs to educate individuals about healthy online habits, critical thinking, and media literacy.

Digital Wellness Workshops: Community workshops and seminars raise awareness about digital well-being and provide practical strategies for achieving a balanced tech-life integration.

5. Collaborative Efforts

Tech Industry Collaboration: Tech companies are partnering to address digital overload collectively, sharing best practices and designing features that prioritize user well-being.

Government Policies: Some governments are introducing regulations and guidelines to promote responsible technology use, especially among younger populations.

Assessing the Impact

The success of these campaigns and interventions is evident through various metrics and indicators, demonstrating the positive changes they have brought about.

1. Behavioral Shifts

Reduced Screen Time: Users who engage with digital detox campaigns or use well-being features report decreased screen time and improved time management.

Increased Mindfulness: Mindfulness and mental health apps have been shown to enhance users' emotional well-being and reduce digital dependency.

2. Improved Mental Health

Stress Reduction: Individuals participating in mindfulness programs or digital wellness workshops report decreased stress levels and better mental health.

Enhanced Focus and Productivity: Users who adopt technology interventions often experience improved focus, leading to enhanced productivity and creativity.

3. Enhanced Relationships

Meaningful Connections: Digital detox initiatives and educational programs have contributed to improved face-to-face interactions and deeper relationships.

Digital Empathy: Users who engage in campaigns promoting digital empathy are more likely to cultivate respectful and considerate online behavior.

Lessons for a Healthier Digital Future

The success of these campaigns and interventions offers valuable lessons for shaping a healthier digital future.

1. Holistic Approach

Addressing digital overload requires a comprehensive approach that encompasses mental, physical, and social aspects of well-being.

2. Technology as a Solution

While technology contributes to digital overload, it can also be leveraged to provide solutions and interventions that promote digital well-being.

3. Collaboration and Advocacy

Successful outcomes are often the result of collaborative efforts involving governments, tech companies, educators, and individuals.

4. Customization and Empowerment

Effective interventions empower individuals to tailor strategies to their unique needs and circumstances, fostering a sense of ownership over their digital well-being.

Conclusion

As the world continues to grapple with the challenges of digital overload, these successful campaigns and interventions offer a ray of hope. By promoting digital well-being through mindfulness, education, collaboration, and thoughtful design, individuals and societies can navigate the digital landscape in a way that enhances their lives rather than detracts from them. The lessons learned from these endeavors serve as a blueprint for creating a healthier and more balanced relationship with technology, ensuring that the digital age contributes positively to both individual health and the well-being of society as a whole.

Chapter 18. Finding Balance in the Digital Era
Strategies for Individuals, Families, and Societies to Cultivate Healthy Tech Habits

Introduction

In today's rapidly evolving digital landscape, technology has become an integral part of our daily lives. From smartphones to social media platforms, digital devices and applications offer unparalleled convenience, connectivity, and information access. However, the widespread use of technology has also brought about challenges, including the potential for digital overload and its impact on both individual well-being and societal dynamics. This article explores the concept of finding balance in the digital era and offers strategies for individuals, families, and societies to cultivate healthy tech habits, ensuring a harmonious coexistence with technology.

Understanding Digital Overload

1. The Digital Overload Dilemma: The rise of smartphones, constant connectivity, and the pervasive presence of screens in our lives have led to a phenomenon known as digital overload. This refers to the overwhelming state individuals experience when they are constantly bombarded by notifications, emails, messages, and other digital stimuli. Digital overload can lead to heightened stress, anxiety, decreased productivity, and strained relationships.

2. The Impact on Health and Society: The effects of digital overload extend beyond personal well-being, affecting societal dynamics. Increased screen time has been linked to

sleep disturbances, eye strain, and sedentary lifestyles, contributing to a range of physical health issues. Additionally, social interactions can be compromised as individuals prioritize virtual connections over face-to-face communication. Addressing these challenges requires a holistic approach that encourages a balanced relationship with technology.

Cultivating Healthy Tech Habits: Strategies for Individuals

1. Mindful Device Usage: **Practicing mindfulness involves being fully present in the moment, which can be applied to technology use. Set specific time limits for checking emails, social media, and other apps. Create designated tech-free zones and times to allow for meaningful offline interactions and relaxation.**

2. Digital Detox: **Periodically disconnect from digital devices to recharge. Consider a weekend retreat or a day without screens. Engage in activities that promote physical activity, creativity, and human connection.**

3. Prioritizing Real-Life Relationships: **Foster in-person interactions by scheduling regular social outings, family meals, and gatherings. Actively engage in conversations, maintaining eye contact and active listening.**

4. Curating Digital Spaces: **Declutter your digital environment by unsubscribing from unnecessary newsletters, organizing apps into folders, and minimizing notifications. Create a virtual space that promotes positivity, learning, and personal growth.**

5. Establishing a Bedtime Routine: **Create a technology-free bedtime routine to improve sleep quality. Avoid**

screens before bedtime and replace screen time with calming activities such as reading, meditation, or gentle stretching.

Nurturing Healthy Tech Habits: Strategies for Families

1. Setting Tech Guidelines: Establish clear and age-appropriate guidelines for tech use within the family. Designate screen-free times, such as during meals and before bedtime. Encourage open discussions about responsible device usage.

2. Family Activities and Bonding: Plan activities that encourage family bonding and limit screen time. Outdoor excursions, board games, cooking together, and shared hobbies promote quality time and strengthen relationships.

3. Tech Education: Educate family members about the potential effects of excessive screen time. Encourage critical thinking and responsible online behavior. Emphasize the importance of privacy, digital etiquette, and distinguishing between credible and unreliable information.

4. Lead by Example: Children often mimic their parents' behaviors. Demonstrate healthy tech habits by modeling balanced technology use and showing that real-life interactions take precedence over screens.

5. Creative Technology Use: Integrate technology into family activities in constructive ways. Collaborate on creative projects, explore educational apps together, and use video calls to connect with distant relatives.

Fostering Healthy Tech Habits: Strategies for Societies

1. Digital Literacy Programs: Implement comprehensive digital literacy programs in schools and communities. Equip individuals with the skills to navigate the digital landscape responsibly, critically assess information, and protect their digital identities.

2. Promoting Digital Wellness Apps: Develop and promote apps designed to help users manage screen time, set goals, and track digital habits. These apps can empower individuals to make informed decisions about their tech usage.

3. Work-Life Balance Initiatives: Encourage workplaces to establish policies that support work-life balance. Flextime, remote work options, and designated "unplugged" hours can contribute to reduced digital overload and increased employee well-being.

4. Redefining Social Norms: Shift societal perceptions around excessive screen time and promote the value of face-to-face interactions. Highlight success stories of individuals and families who have successfully integrated healthy tech habits into their lives.

5. Collaborative Efforts: Government agencies, educational institutions, and technology companies can collaborate to create awareness campaigns and resources that address digital overload. These efforts can highlight the benefits of balanced tech habits and provide tools for individuals and families to implement positive changes.

Conclusion

In the age of digital dominance, finding balance between technology and well-being is a shared responsibility. Individuals, families, and societies must actively engage in cultivating healthy tech habits to mitigate the negative impact of digital overload. By practicing mindfulness, setting boundaries, nurturing real-life relationships, and leveraging technology in meaningful ways, we can create a harmonious coexistence with the digital world. Through collective efforts, we can ensure that the benefits of technology enhance our lives without compromising our physical and mental well-being or the fabric of our societies.

"Impact of Digital Overload on Health and Society" is a comprehensive exploration of the intricate relationship between technology and well-being. This thought-provoking book delves into the evolution of electronic gadgets, scrutinizes the psychological allure behind excessive device use, and delves into pertinent issues such as eye health, sedentary lifestyle, and repetitive strain injuries. Through meticulously researched chapters, it dissects the impact of gadgets on concentration, productivity, and mental health, unraveling the delicate balance between healthy recreation and screen time.

The book examines the effects of technology on self-esteem, identity, cyberbullying, interpersonal relationships, and even love in the digital age. With a critical lens, it assesses the tech industry's role in public health and delves into government policies, culminating in a guide to promoting digital well-being and fostering a harmonious coexistence with technology. A must-read for individuals, families, and societies seeking to navigate the digital landscape while nurturing healthy tech habits.

ABOUT THE AUTHOR

Mr. C. P. Kumar is a retired Scientist 'G' from National Institute of Hydrology, Roorkee, Uttarakhand, India. He is also a Reiki Healer and Chakra Balancing practitioner (with pendulum dowsing) and offers Emotional Freedom Technique (EFT) to help individuals with emotional issues. Mr. Kumar has authored many books on technical, spiritual, and social topics.

For further details, you may visit his webpage
https://www.angelfire.com/nh/cpkumar/virgo.html